LEARN THE VALUE OF

Friendship

◆

by Elaine P. Goley

Illustrated by Debbie Crocker

◆

ROURKE ENTERPRISES, INC.

VERO BEACH, FL 32964

5229646

Library of Congress Cataloging-in-Publication Data

Goley, Elaine P., 1949–
    Learn the value of friendship.

    Summary: Presents situations that demonstrate
the meaning and importance of friendship.
    1. Friendship—Juvenile literature. [1. Friendship.
2. Conduct of life] I. Title. II. Title: Friendship.
BJ1533.F8G57 1987   177′.6   87-16288
ISBN 0-86592-376-0

Friendship

Do you know what **friendship** is?

Sharing your sandwich with someone who forgot
his lunch is **friendship.**

Friendship is telling someone its dangerous to play in the street.

Letting someone borrow your favorite toy
is **friendship.**

When you visit someone who broke her leg and can't come out to play, that's **friendship**.

Helping your sister with her math homework
is **friendship.**

When you share your new blocks with someone,
that's **friendship.**

Friendship is going with your friend to a movie
you have already seen.

Feeding your neighbor's cat while she's away
is **friendship.**

When you let someone play with your favorite puzzle, that's **friendship.**

Friendship is helping your friend finish cleaning the garage so that you can play ball.

Telling someone that you think she's special
is **friendship.**

Sharing your last chocolate chip cookie
is **friendship.**

When you help your neighbor weed her garden,
that's **friendship.**

Friendship is telling someone that he played well
at his piano recital.

When you draw a special picture for someone
because she's not feeling well, that's **friendship.**

Letting someone read your new book is **friendship.**

Friendship is showing others you care about them.

Friendship

"How would you like to spend a few nights at Amy's house?" asked Jenny's mom.

"Wow, can I, Mom?" asked Jenny.

"Amy and Mrs. Smith said to come over today," said Jenny's mom. "Hurry and pack."

Jenny and Amy played all afternoon with their dolls. They ate dinner and watched TV for a while.

"Time for bed," said Mrs. Smith.

The girls washed up, brushed their teeth, and hopped into bed.

Amy hugged her teddy bear and closed her eyes. She heard Jenny crying.

"What's the matter, Jen?" asked Amy.

"I miss my family. And I forgot to pack my fluffy dog," Jenny said.

"Take my teddy bear," said Amy. "He's soft and friendly."

How did Amy show **friendship**?
What would you have done if you were Amy?

Friendship

Ann was having a birthday party. Kim, David, Mary, Bob, and Ted, brought her gifts. The children played tag and ran races. Then they sat at the picnic table. Ann's mom brought out a big cake.

"Happy birthday to you," sang the children.

The children heard a loud noise. They saw a big truck pull into the driveway next door. Men took some big chairs off the truck and carried them into the house.

"Look, someone is moving in," said Ann.

A car pulled up in front of the house. A boy about Ann's age hopped out. He looked at Ann and her friends. He waved to them.

"Hi," said the boy. "My name is Harry."

Ann and her friends looked at one another. But they didn't say a word.

Who was showing **friendship?**

What would you have done if you were at Ann's party?